Lerner SPORTS

SUPER SPORTS
TEAMS

T0004427

INSIDE THE
KANSAS CITY
CHIEFS

JOSH ANDERSON

Lerner Publications ◆ Minneapolis

SPORTS THRILLS MEET RESEARCH SKILLS

Lerner SPORTS

Free Database Trial: **lernersports.com**

Lerner Publications Company
An imprint of Lerner Publishing Group, Inc.
241 First Avenue North
Minneapolis, MN 55401 USA

For reading levels and more information, look up this title at www.lernerbooks.com.

Main body text set in Aptifer Slab LT Pro / Typeface provided by Linotype AG

Library of Congress Cataloging-in-Publication Data

Names: Anderson, Josh, author.
Title: Inside the Kansas City Chiefs / Josh Anderson.
Description: Minneapolis, MN: Lerner Publications , [2024] | Series: Lerner sports. Super sports teams | Includes bibliographical references and index. | Audience: Ages 7–11 | Audience: Grades 4–6 | Summary: "Quarterback Patrick Mahomes makes the Kansas City Chiefs one of the hottest teams in the NFL. See what the future holds for the team that has played in two of the past three Super Bowls"— Provided by publisher.
Identifiers: LCCN 2022048444 (print) | LCCN 2022048445 (ebook) | ISBN 9781728491004 (library binding) | ISBN 9798765604038 (paperback) | ISBN 9798765601556 (ebook)
Subjects: LCSH: Kansas City Chiefs (Football team) —History—Juvenile literature.
Classification: LCC GV956.K35 A64 2024 (print) | LCC GV956.K35 (ebook) | DDC 796.332/6409778411—dc23/ eng/20221017

LC record available at https://lccn.loc.gov/20220484f44
LC ebook record available at https://lccn.loc.gov/2022048445

Manufactured in the United States of America
1 – CG – 7/15/23

TABLE OF CONTENTS

Patrick Mahomes (*center*) throws the ball during the 2020 Super Bowl.

THE LEGION OF ZOOM

FACTS AT A GLANCE

- The **KANSAS CITY CHIEFS** first played in Texas and were called the Dallas Texans.

- The Chiefs won their first **SUPER BOWL** in 1970, defeating the Minnesota Vikings 23–7.

- The Chiefs chose quarterback **PATRICK MAHOMES** with the 10th overall pick of the 2017 National Football League (NFL) Draft.

- Kansas City's **565 POINTS** in 2018 are the third most ever scored by an NFL team in one season.

- **KANSAS CITY** came back from 10 points down in the fourth quarter to win the 2020 Super Bowl.

The Kansas City Chiefs were playing the San Francisco 49ers in the 2020 Super Bowl. The Chiefs were looking for their first Super Bowl title in 50 years. The team's fans were hungry for a victory.

The Chiefs were one of the highest-scoring teams in the NFL during the regular season. They could score points so quickly that fans called them The Legion of Zoom. But San Francisco's powerful defense held Kansas City to only one touchdown in the first three quarters. When the Chiefs started a drive with around nine minutes to play in the fourth quarter, they trailed 20–10.

Facing third down with 15 yards to go, Chiefs quarterback Patrick Mahomes needed to make a big play. He looked for an open receiver. Four defenders rushed toward him. Mahomes launched the ball high into the air toward Tyreek Hill, his top wide receiver. One of the fastest players in the NFL, Hill streaked up the middle of the field and toward the left sideline. He grabbed the ball just before three San Francisco players dragged him to the ground. The incredible play gained the Chiefs 44 yards and led to a touchdown a few plays later.

The Chiefs scored two more times in the final minutes of the game and defeated the 49ers 31–20. Fans in Kansas City could finally celebrate their first Super Bowl victory since 1970. For leading the incredible comeback, Mahomes won the game's Most Valuable Player (MVP) award.

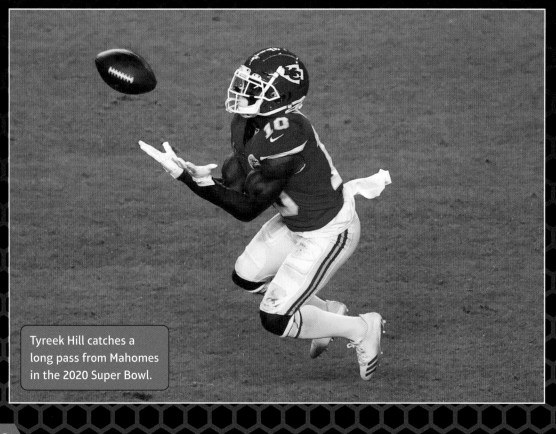

Tyreek Hill catches a long pass from Mahomes in the 2020 Super Bowl.

Since Mahomes became the team's quarterback, the Chiefs have never missed the playoffs.

Quarterback Len Dawson in his Chiefs uniform. He played one season for the Dallas Texans and 13 seasons for the Kansas City Chiefs.

GUARDIANS OF ARROWHEAD

When the Chiefs began playing in 1960, they were called the Dallas Texans. Lamar Hunt was their first owner. Hunt helped create the American Football League (AFL), and the Texans were one of the AFL's first teams. The Texans played home games at the Cotton Bowl in Dallas, Texas. In 1962, the Texans added quarterback Len Dawson. In Dawson's first season in Dallas, he led the team to the AFL Championship Game.

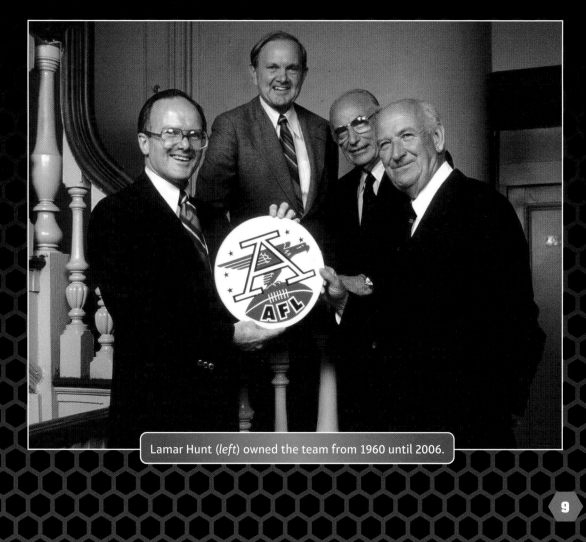

Lamar Hunt (*left*) owned the team from 1960 until 2006.

In a battle of two teams from the same state, the Texans played against the Houston Oilers for the AFL Championship. The Texans took a 17–0 lead in the first half. But the Oilers tied the score in the second half and the game went into overtime. Neither team scored in the first overtime period. Finally, Tommy Brooker kicked a 25-yard field goal in the second overtime. The Texans won 20–17.

In 1963, the team moved to Kansas City, Missouri. Hunt changed the team's name to honor Kansas City's mayor, Roe "Chief" Bartle. The Chiefs began playing at Arrowhead Stadium in 1972. The stadium is still the team's home.

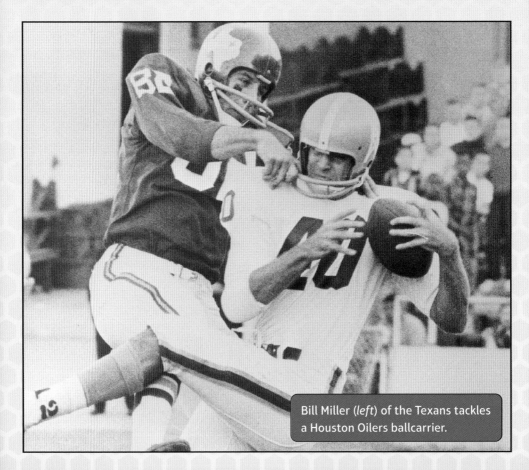

Bill Miller (*left*) of the Texans tackles a Houston Oilers ballcarrier.

CHIEFS FACT

In 1970, Hank Stram became the first head coach to wear a microphone during the Super Bowl. The microphone allowed fans to hear what the coach said to his players during the game.

Arrowhead Stadium can hold more than 76,000 fans on game days.

In 1967, the Chiefs played in the first Super Bowl. The game was the first time the AFL's champion had a chance to play against the best team in the NFL. Kansas City's opponent was the Green Bay Packers. Led by legendary coach Vince Lombardi, the Packers won the game 35–10.

The Chiefs built a 16–0 lead in the first half of the 1970 Super Bowl against the Minnesota Vikings.

Kansas City's coach at the time was Hank Stram. No coach in the team's history has led Kansas City to more wins. Stram and quarterback Len Dawson took the Chiefs to the Super Bowl again three years later. Their opponent in 1970 was the Minnesota Vikings. The Vikings were the top scoring team and had the best defense in the NFL that season. Most people thought the Vikings would win the game.

The Chiefs surprised many people when they overpowered the Vikings. Kansas City held Minnesota scoreless for the game's first half. The Chiefs defense forced three interceptions in the game and sacked Minnesota's quarterback three times. The Chiefs won the game 23–7. Dawson won the 1970 Super Bowl MVP award.

Hank Stram was the team's first head coach. During his 15 seasons, he led them to three championships.

Legendary quarterback Joe Montana played the final two seasons of his career for the Chiefs.

AMAZING MOMENTS

After their victory in the 1970 Super Bowl, the Chiefs only made the playoffs twice over the next 20 seasons. In 1989, the team hired coach Marty Schottenheimer. Schottenheimer turned the team around. He led the Chiefs to six straight playoff appearances from 1990 to 1995. During two of those seasons, Kansas City's quarterback was Joe Montana. Montana is one of the greatest quarterbacks of all time. He led the San Francisco 49ers to four Super Bowl victories before joining the Chiefs in 1993.

Marty Schottenheimer ranks seventh in NFL history with 200 coaching victories.

From 1998 to 2012, the Chiefs made the playoffs three times. But they did not win any of their playoff games. In 2013, the team hired Andy Reid as its head coach. Even though Reid led the Chiefs to the playoffs four times in his first five years in Kansas City, the team only won one playoff game during that time.

The Chiefs chose quarterback Patrick Mahomes with the 10th overall pick in the 2017 NFL Draft. Mahomes became the team's starting quarterback in 2018 and led Kansas City to a 12–4 record. In only the third start of his career, Mahomes had one of the best performances ever for an NFL quarterback. He threw six touchdown passes and no interceptions in a 42–37 victory over the Pittsburgh Steelers. The Chiefs scored 565 points in 2018. Only the Denver Broncos and New England Patriots have scored more points in a single season.

The team earned a spot in the 2019 American Football Conference (AFC)

Mahomes threw 151 touchdown passes during his first four seasons as the team's starting quarterback.

Championship Game. If they could beat the Patriots, they would go to the Super Bowl. The game took place at Arrowhead Stadium. The Chiefs came from behind in the fourth quarter to tie the game 31–31. But the Patriots had Tom Brady, the most successful quarterback of all time. They won the game in overtime.

The following season, the Chiefs won their first Super Bowl in 50 years when they defeated the San Francisco 49ers. The Chiefs made it back to the Super Bowl again in 2021. They lost to the Tampa Bay Buccaneers. But the very next season, Kansas City returned to the Super Bowl. This time, they defeated the Philadelphia Eagles 38–35. Patrick Mahomes won the Super Bowl MVP for the second time.

Running back Damien Williams (*right*) catches a touchdown pass against the New England Patriots in the 2019 AFC Championship Game.

Linebacker Derrick Thomas (*right*) sacks Indianapolis Colts quarterback Jim Harbaugh.

CHIEFS SUPERSTARS

Many incredible players have worn a Chiefs uniform. Len Dawson played 14 seasons for the team. He led the AFL in touchdown passes four times. The Chiefs won 93 regular season games during Dawson's career.

Dawson was a Pro Bowl player seven times.

Pro Football Hall of Famer Derrick Thomas was one of the best linebackers ever to play football. He was part of the team from 1989 to 1999. Thomas was skilled at pressuring the opposing team's quarterback. He led the league with 20 sacks in 1990. Offensive lineman Will Shields never missed a game because of injury in his 14-year career. The Hall of Famer played in the Pro Bowl 12 times.

Running back Christian Okoye was born in Nigeria. He earned the nickname the Nigerian Nightmare for his powerful running style and ability to break through tackles. He led the NFL in rushing with 1,480 yards in 1989.

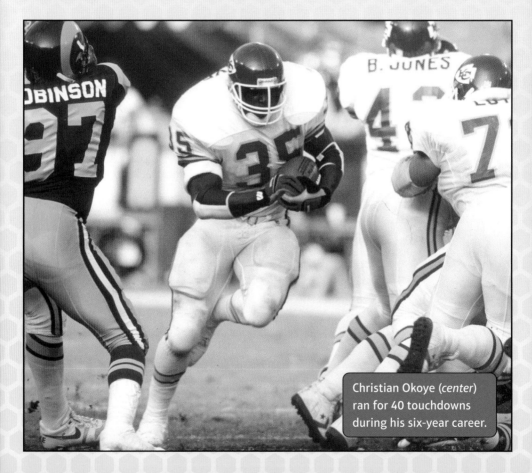

Christian Okoye (*center*) ran for 40 touchdowns during his six-year career.

CHIEFS FACT

In 1967, Kansas City quarterback Len Dawson became the first player to complete a pass in the Super Bowl.

In 2001, Priest Holmes (*top*) led the NFL with 1,555 rushing yards.

Only one other player has scored more rushing touchdowns in a season than running back Priest Holmes has. In 2003, Holmes ran for 27 touchdowns. He scored 83 total touchdowns in 65 games with the Chiefs from 2001 to 2007.

Tony Gonzalez is one of the greatest tight ends in NFL history. Gonzalez finished his career with 15,127 receiving yards. That's the sixth most receiving yards in league history. And it's more than any other tight end has totaled. The Hall of Famer was a Pro Bowl player 14 times during his NFL career.

Tyreek Hill scored 62 touchdowns during his six seasons with the Chiefs.

Wide receiver Tyreek Hill was a Pro Bowl player after all six of his seasons with the Chiefs. He finished with more than 1,000 receiving yards four times. Hill is one of the fastest runners in the NFL.

In his first year as Kansas City's starting quarterback, Patrick Mahomes threw 50 touchdowns and only 12 interceptions. He won the 2018 NFL MVP award. Mahomes led the Chiefs to the AFC Championship Game in each of his first five seasons as a starter. In three of those seasons, the Chiefs made it to the Super Bowl.

Tight end Travis Kelce has played in the Pro Bowl seven times. He had six 1,000-yard seasons in a row from 2016 to 2021. Kelce caught a touchdown in the fourth quarter of the 2020 Super Bowl, helping the Chiefs seal their comeback victory.

Travis Kelce (*left*) caught four touchdowns during a 2022 game, one short of the NFL record for tight ends.

Mahomes is not the first professional athlete in his family. His father was a Major League Baseball player.

LET'S GO, CHIEFS!

After back-to-back trips to the Super Bowl, the Chiefs almost made it back again in 2022. In their fourth-straight AFC Championship Game, the Chiefs faced off against the Cincinnati Bengals. Kansas City led 21–10 at halftime. But the Bengals came back and won the game in overtime.

Coach Reid has led Kansas City to the playoffs for eight straight seasons. To help keep the streak going, the team has two of the best players in the NFL. Mahomes is one of the league's top quarterbacks. If the rest of his career goes the way his first few seasons have, Mahomes may one day be considered the greatest quarterback of all time. Travis Kelce holds multiple NFL records, including the most single-season receiving yards as a tight end. Kelce was also the first tight end in NFL history to have 100 or more catches in more than one season.

Andy Reid coached the Philadelphia Eagles for 14 seasons before coming to Kansas City in 2013.

The team also added some new players to help the team score. Before the 2022 season, wide receivers JuJu Smith-Schuster and Marquez Valdes-Scantling signed with the Chiefs.

On defense, the Chiefs have one of the best defensive lines in the league. Defensive tackle Chris Jones was a Pro Bowl player each season from 2019 to 2021. Another Pro Bowl player, Frank Clark, will pair with 2022 first-round draft pick George Karlaftis. The two defensive ends will work to make life difficult for opposing quarterbacks.

After an amazing season, the Chiefs played in their fifth Super Bowl in 2023 and won a third title. With plenty of new and returning talent, fans in Kansas City know the sky's the limit for the Chiefs.

JuJu Smith-Schuster had 79 receiving yards in his first game for the Chiefs in 2022.

Defensive tackle Chris Jones ranked third in the NFL with 15.5 sacks in 2018.

CHIEFS
SEASON RECORD
HOLDERS

RUSHING TOUCHDOWNS

1. Priest Holmes, 27 (2003)
2. Priest Holmes, 21 (2002)
3. Larry Johnson, 20 (2005)
4. Larry Johnson, 17 (2006)
5. Priest Holmes, 14 (2004)

RECEIVING TOUCHDOWNS

1. Dwayne Bowe, 15 (2010)
   Tyreek Hill, 15 (2020)
2. Chris Burford, 12 (1962)
   Tyreek Hill, 12 (2018)
   Travis Kelce, 12 (2022)
3. Otis Taylor, 11 (1967)
   Stephone Paige, 11 (1986)
   Tony Gonzalez, 11 (1999)
   Travis Kelce, 11 (2020)

PASSING YARDS

1. Patrick Mahomes, 5,250 (2022)
2. Patrick Mahomes, 5,097 (2018)
3. Patrick Mahomes, 4,839 (2021)
4. Patrick Mahomes, 4,740 (2020)
5. Trent Green, 4,591 (2004)

RUSHING YARDS

1. Larry Johnson, 1,789 (2006)
2. Larry Johnson, 1,750 (2005)
3. Priest Holmes, 1,615 (2002)
4. Priest Holmes, 1,555 (2001)
5. Jamaal Charles, 1,509 (2012)

PASS COMPLETIONS

1. Patrick Mahomes, 436 (2021)
2. Patrick Mahomes, 435 (2022)
3. Patrick Mahomes, 390 (2020)
4. Patrick Mahomes, 383 (2018)
5. Trent Green, 369 (2004)

SACKS

1. Justin Houston, 22 (2014)
2. Derrick Thomas, 20 (1990)
3. Jared Allen, 15.5 (2007)
   Chris Jones, 15.5 (2018)
   Chris Jones, 15.5 (2022)
4. Neil Smith, 15 (1993)

GLOSSARY

conference: a group of sports teams that play against one another

defensive end: a player whose main jobs are to rush the quarterback and defend rushing plays

draft: when teams take turns choosing new players

drive: a series of plays by the offense in a football game

field goal: three points scored when the football is kicked between the goalposts

linebacker: a defender who usually plays in the middle of the defense

overtime: an extra period of play to decide a winner when the game is tied

playoffs: extra games after a season to determine the champion in a sport

Pro Bowl: the NFL's all-star game

sack: when the quarterback is tackled for a loss of yards

tight end: a player whose main jobs are to block and catch passes

LEARN MORE

Berglund, Bruce. *Football GOATs: The Greatest Athletes of All Time*. North Mankato, MN: Capstone Publishing, 2022.

Fishman, Jon M. *Patrick Mahomes*. Minneapolis: Lerner Publications, 2019.

Kansas City Chiefs
https://www.chiefs.com/

Pro Football Hall of Fame: Kansas City Chiefs
https://www.profootballhof.com/Teams/kansas-city-chiefs

Sports Illustrated Kids—Football
https://www.sikids.com/football

Wetzel, Dan. *Epic Athletes: Patrick Mahomes*. New York: Henry Holt and Company, 2020.

INDEX

PHOTO ACKNOWLEDGMENTS

Image credits: Focus On Sport/Contributor/Getty Images, p.4; Elsa/Staff/ Getty Images, p.6; Focus On Sport/Contributor/Getty Images, p.7; Diamond Images/Contributor/Getty Images, p.8; Ross Lewis/Contributor/Getty Images, p.9; Bettmann/Contributor/Getty Images, p.10; Denver Post/Contributor/ Getty Images, p.11; Focus On Sport/Contributor/Getty Images, p.12; Focus On Sport/Contributor/Getty Images, p.13; The Sporting News/Contributor/Getty Images, p.14; George Gojkovich/Contributor/Getty Images, p.15; Jamie Squire/ Staff/Getty Images, p.16; David Eulitt/Contributor/Getty Images, p.17; PETER NEWCOMB/Staff/Getty Images, p.18; Focus On Sport/Contributor/Getty Images, p.19; Focus On Sport/Contributor/Getty Images, p.20; Sporting News Archive/ Contributor/Getty Images, p.21; Jamie Squire/Staff/Getty Images, p.22; Michael Hickey/Contributor/Getty Images, p.23; Jamie Squire/Staff/Getty Images, p.24; Michael Hickey/Contributor/Getty Images, p.25; Michael Hickey/Contributor/ Getty Images, p.26; David Eulitt/Contributor/Getty Images, p.27; Robert B. Stanton/Stringer/Getty Images, p.28

Design element: Master3D/Shutterstock.com.

Cover image: Rob Carr/Staff/Getty Images